RESCUE SERVICES

TWENTIETH-CENTURY DEVELOPMENTS IN FASHION AND COSTUME

RESCUE SERVICES

CAROL HARRIS AND MIKE BROWN

MASON CREST PUBLISHERS

www.masoncrest.com

Mason Crest Publishers Inc.
370 Reed Road
Broomall, PA 19008
(866) MCP-BOOK (toll free)
www.masoncrest.com

First printing 2002

1 2 3 4 5 6 7 8 9 10

Library of Congress Cataloging-in-Publication Data available

ISBN 1-59084-428-9

Printed and bound in Malaysia

Editorial and design by
Amber Books Ltd.
Bradley's Close
74–77 White Lion Street
London N1 9PF

Project Editor: Marie-Claire Muir
Designer: Zoe Mellors
Picture Research: Lisa Wren

Picture Credits:
Amber Books Ltd: 5 (left and bottom right), 14. **Mike Brown:** 37. **The Culture Archive:** 10. **Kobal:** 39. **London Ambulance Service:** 35. **Mary Evans Picture Library:** 12, 26. **Popperfoto:** 8, 16, 19, 20, 23, 28, 33, 36, 42, 45, 49. **Topham:** 5 (top right), 9, 24, 25, 31, 46, 52, 57, 59. **U.S. Coast Guard:** 6, 44, 51, 54, 56.

Cover images: **The Culture Archive:** bottom left. **Topham:** background, main, and top left.

Acknowledgment:
For authenticating this book, the Publishers would like to thank
JONES NEW YORK

Contents

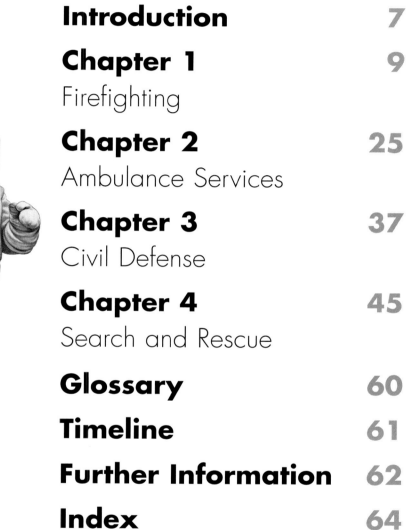

CHAPTER 1

Firefighting

One of the oldest rescue services in the United States is the fire service. Benjamin Franklin set up the first volunteer fire department in Philadelphia in 1735. From its basic beginnings, the service became increasingly sophisticated, especially in the 20th century, as did firefighters' protective clothing.

The beginning of the 20th century witnessed one of the world's most significant technological revolutions: the introduction of motor engines and the various vehicles powered by them. Consequences were many and far-reaching, and one of them was the phasing-out of the fire service's old horse-drawn pumps, although in some rural areas, these continued to be used well after World War I.

Three hotshots (left) fight a raging bushfire. They wear hard hats with eye shields and headphones. Today's firefighter often wears a full-protective suit, including the one shown here (right) rescuing a toddler.

During the 1920s, pneumatic (air-filled) tires replaced the old solid-rubber versions, and new engines were built fully enclosed, unlike the earlier open models. Both of these advances made the firefighters' job less uncomfortable and even safer. In the 1930s, they tried to install the first radios in fire engines, but early radios were extremely big, which made them impractical. However, by the 1940s, the invention of **walkie-talkies** improved the job of the firemen.

EARLY UNIFORMS

Firefighters work in extremes—incredibly high heat, flames, and water constantly soaking them, either cascading from above or splashing back at them. Their work clothes have to protect them in these situations, and more.

Wearing soaking wet clothes in the winter is extremely cold; as one former firefighter put it, "You were either freezing cold or roasting, and always soaked to the skin!"

Early protective clothing was similar to that used by mariners or serious fishermen: oilskin overcoat and overtrousers, with rubber boots or thigh-length **waders**. Uniforms, too, were often based on those of seamen. In many places, ex-sailors were preferred as firemen—it was felt that they were used to working with water, as well as

This early 20th-century firefighter wears a brass cavalry-style helmet and a military-type uniform with brass buttons. This dress is typical of many European and some American firefighters of this period.

HELMETS

At the beginning of the 20th century, French and British firemen's helmets were, in many cases, based on the crested helmets French cavalry regiments wore. This is because a regiment of the French Army called the Sapeurs Pompiers (pump engineers) was specially trained to fight fires. These men wore the tall brass helmets of the French Army, and it was from them that the use of these helmets spread. In military terms, they were more for show than protection, and as such, were highly ornate.

working for long periods soaked to the skin—and former Navy or Army officers were often appointed to run the local service. Uniforms were usually in nautical dark blue, with pea jackets and naval-type peaked caps. Firemen of the London Fire Brigade, for instance, wore naval ratings-style peakless caps until the 1940s. The alternative color to blue was red, signifying fire; this was often incorporated into the uniform as **piping**, **epaulets**, or other trim.

Like sailors' clothes, firemen's uniforms were of thick material. They gave the wearer some protection from the constant wet, the heat, and the cold, although they were not very comfortable and weighed a lot, especially when wet.

Volunteer firefighters sometimes wore the most amazingly colorful uniforms. One example from Houston consisted of a crimson-red tailcoat with black lapels and cuffs, worn with a red vest, black trousers, a white belt, a blue fire helmet, and—believe it or not—a white bow tie.

One difference from naval uniform was, of course, the helmet, necessary to protect the wearer from falling debris that might be on fire. Although they were for practical use, early firemen's helmets were often in an ornate style; like the buttons on firemen's **tunics**, they were usually made of brass—a practical measure, because they would not rust, an important consideration for uniforms

In this British World War II poster, the tommy helmet and gas mask on the firefighter's chest give away the wartime date. Notice the long rubber waders, the ax on his belt, and the early oxygen tanks on his back.

that would regularly get soaking wet. However, a new invention was to change helmet design. Electricity was being installed in houses and other buildings, and in the event of fire, live electric cables were often hanging down dangerously; one touch of those on a metal helmet could prove fatal for the fireman wearing it. A safer alternative was needed, and fiber, or the fast-developing new plastics, held the answer; helmets made of these would provide protection from falling rubble and electric shock. Other alternatives included a return to leather helmets, or even cork.

German fire helmets were similar to the German Army "coal scuttle" helmet, but with a crest that ran up the back and over the top. Like other fire helmets of the time, they could be fitted with a leather curtain, which hung down the back and sides of the helmet to protect the neck—and helped stop water from trickling down inside the collar.

By the beginning of the 20th century, most U.S. firefighters' helmets had already taken on the form that is familiar today. Painted leather shields—also called hat fronts—mounted on the front of the fire helmet were used to identify the fire company and rank of the wearer. Some of them were quite colorful.

Many firemen still carried one piece of metal insignia—a badge of some sort that identified them, either by name or number, so that, if they were caught by the fire or buried under the rubble, their bodies could be identified.

PERSONAL EQUIPMENT

One of the earliest pieces of personal equipment firefighters carried is still with us today: the hand ax, which is very useful for making an entrance into a blazing but locked building, to help free trapped people, or for dozens of other small jobs. These hung from the thick belts that firemen wore around their waists, along with two other pieces of personal equipment—a hose wrench, to attach hoses to hydrants, and a rolled-up hemp line, to fasten a ladder to a building, a hose, or the firefighter himself to the ladder.

One other piece of personal equipment, for fire chiefs only, was the speaking trumpet through which they shouted orders to the firefighters. These were sometimes quite elaborately decorated.

FIREFIGHTERS IN WORLD WAR II

Firefighters in World War II had to deal not only with ordinary fires, but also with fires caused by enemy bombing, especially incendiary (fire) bombs. This meant that, in addition to facing the dangers of the fire itself, they had to take account of falling bombs. In Britain, during the Blitz, a period of relentless bombing by the Germans, the firemen wore British Army steel helmets painted gray, with leather curtains to protect their necks.

A serious shortage of manpower meant that women were taken into the fire service in large numbers. They often worked in control rooms, but they also helped to fight fires. They wore a blue uniform consisting of a long tunic with four pockets, a knee-length skirt or ski pants, and a ski cap. A badge worn on the cap and the left breast pocket or arm bore the letters "AFS" (Auxiliary Fire Service) or "NFS" (National Fire Service).

GROUNDCREW FIREFIGHTING UNIT, ROYAL AIR FORCE
Malaya 1945

Firefighting was a tremendously dangerous job for air force personnel, because airfields and aircraft usually have copious amounts of ammunition, aviation fuel, kerosene, and other flammable substances present. This RAF man wears the full protective suit designed for tackling chronic fires, made from asbestos and with full-body coverage and the minimum of joints that might be wrenched open by blast. The asbestos jacket is double-breasted and secured with a metal clasp and a chain. The trousers cover the entire foot and are rubber soled at the bottom. Elbow-length gloves give substantial protection to the hands. Headgear is a large hood zipped into place, and vision is provided through a tinted and reinforced glass plate at the front. This firefighting clothing was issued to RAF units at home and abroad.

MODERN UNIFORMS

The trend during the 20th century has been for uniforms, or at least the uniform worn while fighting fires, to become as practical as possible. One of the factors that has made this possible is the development of new, manmade fibers, which first appeared in the mid-20th century. Today, many firefighting suits are made from Nomex, a fire- and heat-resistant fabric, or combinations of Nomex and Kevlar, a hard material used for the manufacture of bulletproof vests. Often, this is mixed with a static-resistant material—a sudden spark caused by a buildup of static electricity might easily ignite flammable chemicals or gases.

A second area of protection that modern designers have worked on is high visibility. Modern fabrics can be produced in fluorescent colors—yellow, lime green, and so forth—which can be augmented by light-reflecting strips or patches. Both make the wearer far more visible in the dust, smoke, and possible darkness of fire scenes, and, therefore, make them safer.

The outer layer of servicewear consists of a long, heavy, waterproof overjacket and pants or coverall, worn with heavy rubber boots and gloves, which typically have cowhide palm and finger pieces for grip and strength and Kevlar/Nomex backs for heat resistance. Because these clothes themselves are hot to wear—added to the hot work of fighting fires—many firefighters wear only t-shirts and shorts under their protective clothing. Finally, there is the helmet, which is often brightly colored to indicate rank or specialization for easy recognition.

Service uniforms, as described, are designed with an emphasis on practicality. Conversely, dress uniforms, worn for ceremonial or formal occasions, are designed for show and are usually far more traditional and military in style. Each fire department has its own design, and there are many variations, most being either dark blue and similar to police uniforms, or the light brown often called chino, similar to U.S. Army summer uniforms.

There is a third uniform variation, called station dress. This is what is worn at the fire station in between fire callouts. It often consists of a short- or long-sleeved shirt, typically with two flapped breast pockets and epaulets, all in fire-service navy blue. Trousers, also in navy blue, have two front **welt** pockets, plus two in the rear. With this might be worn a firefighter's heavy-duty, long-sleeved, front-zippered **blouson jacket**, also in navy.

These modern firefighters are wearing lightweight plastic helmets with clear face shields. They are using high-visibility reflective strips and are wearing badges with the word "FIRE" on their coats and trousers.

Badges

Outer service clothing, coveralls, and waterproof overjacket almost always have the name or initials of the fire department on the back, for example "FDNY" (New York Fire Department). However, station clothes and dress uniform might have state badges, local badges, or specialist insignia, usually sewn onto the upper arm or chest.

The badges come in all shapes and colors. Many bear a device, such as a fire helmet imposed on a crossed hose nozzle, ladder, pole hook, or ax. One example is shaped like a **Maltese cross** in white edged with red, with the device described in the center, with the words "FIRE" above and "DEPT" below, a hydrant on the right, and a ladder on the left. Others have an embroidered version of a silver or gold shield, or a black shield with a gold American eagle in the center, and the words "FIRE DEPT." above in gold, with a scroll in white below to hold the name of the town.

There are many more types, such as for ladies auxiliary, hazardous materials team, extrication technician, or volunteer fire department. One common badge is for first aid or emergency medical technician. During the 1950s and 1960s, it was realized that the sooner casualties received medical attention, the likelier they were to recover. Like all other rescue services, firefighters now routinely receive first-aid training.

Those who have received advanced training often wear badges signifying their specialist status. One example shows a blue **star of life** bearing a yellow snake, all in a white circle, set in a black shield with a yellow border with the words "FIRE DEPT." above and "EMT" (Emergency Medical Technician) below, all in yellow letters, or, alternatively, the word "PARAMEDIC" below.

Modern Helmets

Modern U.S. firefighters' helmets are either made with a heat-resistant thermoplastic outer shell, which has high penetration and impact resistance, or made from fiberglass, which is resistant to chemical attack and remains stable in extreme heat. They have a urethane foam liner to give protection from impact, and can be fitted with half- or full-face clear plastic face shields. Other optional fittings include earphones and a neck protector—a curtain of material, made of a heat-resistant fiber such as Nomex, that hangs down from the sides and rear of the helmet.

American firefighters also have a modern version of the helmet shield at the front. It usually bears a number in the center identifying the company. Above this is a helmet crescent, with lettering that gives other information about the wearer (rank, specialty, etc.). One manufacturer produces over 30 variations, including chief, crew chief, deputy fire marshal, fire brigade, firefighter, EMT firefighter, fire medic, fire police, fire rescue, hazmat (hazardous materials) team, and paramedic firefighter.

A variation is the modern **air pack**, something like a motorcycle helmet with an integral face mask and air tanks carried on the firefighter's back. Many European fire forces routinely use similar helmets.

HOTSHOTS

As equipment has improved, the training needed to use it has become more intensive. Modern fire departments have to deal with all different types of fires, so there is a need for specialist firefighters.

Especially in long, hot, dry spells, open country is vulnerable to wildfires. These fires can cover vast areas and destroy thousands of acres of woodland or scrubland. Forest-fire specialists are known as hotshots. Many of the national forests and parks in the U.S. maintain 20-man fire crews throughout the summer, which are on call to be sent to forest fires anywhere in the country.

For firefighting, these hotshots wear clothes much more suitable to the woods than ordinary firefighters' clothes. For example, the Prescott National Forest hotshots wear yellow shirts with pouch pockets and long sleeves, green trousers in a shade known as forest-service spruce, and red hard hats. When not fighting fires, they wear green shirts and caps. The New Jersey crew wears a similar outfit, but with yellow hard hats.

Alternatives include zipper-fronted coveralls in high-visibility yellow with reflective strips on the arms and legs, or zipper-fronted long coats, also with reflective strips, with four patch-pockets and made from flame-resistant material.

This picture clearly demonstrates the effectiveness of the high-visibility strips on these modern U.S. firefighters' clothing. Note the similarity between the basic uniforms of U.S., British (p.16), and German (p.20) firefighters.

Different teams are also distinguishable by their badges. The Colorado Wildfire Team, for example, has a badge showing the head of a snarling wildcat, and around it, the legend "285 THE WILDCATS." The Wisconsin Forest Firefighters wear a badge showing their logo, "Torchy," a flame cartoon character carrying a shovel.

Wildfire crews wear special helmets that are similar to construction workers' hard hats. They come in two styles: a round pot-shaped helmet with an all-

A member of the modern German Feuerwehr (Fire Service), the man on the left is wearing a hazmat (hazardous materials) suit, while a second member (center) is in standard uniform. The helmet has a central crest for added strength.

around brim, and one known as a cap, shaped somewhat like a baseball cap. Firefighters' hard hats are made of heat-resistant thermoplastic and fitted with clips for holding goggles or face shields. Another option is the helmet shroud, a sort of tube of heat-resistant material that goes over the head and neck and attaches inside the rim of the hard hat at the back and sides, leaving a small slit at the front through which the hotshot can see.

Among their personal equipment are personal radios used for reporting the progress of the fire and calling for reinforcements, and for directing the aircraft that drop water or fire-retardant substances, which can be highly effective in stopping or slowing runaway wildfires.

SMOKE JUMPERS

There are some specialist forest firefighters who parachute down into the scene of a forest fire while it is still relatively small. These are known as smoke jumpers. Great skill is required if they are not to be badly injured by landing either in the trees or in the fire itself. First, their heavy equipment is dropped by parachute, then the smoke jumpers follow. Sometimes they have to land among the trees— a risky operation, because it is easy to be injured by the branches.

This specialty began in the early decades of the 20th century. Not long after the end of World War I in 1918, the Chief Forester of the U.S. Forest Service, Henry S. Graves, contacted the Chief of the Army Air Service (later known as the Army Air Corps), inquiring about the possibility of cooperation between the two services for the purpose of providing aerial fire detection over some of the forests in the western United States. Soon after World War I, aircraft began to be used to spot forest fires, and some Forest Service officials began thinking about dropping firefighters by parachute; the idea was discarded, however, as being too dangerous. Service personnel from Chelan National Forest in Washington made jumps for the first time in 1939. One of these was Walt Anderson, Chief of Fire Control at Chelan, and it was he who coined the term "smoke jumper."

Luckily, there were no serious injuries. The first operational use of smoke jumpers was made in 1940.

Early smoke jumpers' outfits included a 30-foot (91-cm) backpack chute and a 27-foot (82-cm) emergency chest-pack chute. To provide protection from the hazards of jumping into tree-covered terrain, clothing included a two-piece felt-padded suit, with a pocket on one leg to hold a rope for letting themselves down from trees and other obstacles; a football helmet with a wire-mesh face mask to protect the face when landing among trees; an athletic supporter, ankle braces, and a wide leather and elastic belt to protect against back and abdominal injuries; and heavy logger boots.

Today's smoke jumpers still wear a wire-net mask, only now it is part of a strong thermoplastic jump helmet. Heavy overalls make up the main part of the parachute suit, now made of modern manmade fibers. Underneath, their basic clothes are the same as for hotshots.

Smoke jumpers, too, have distinctive badges. The smokejumpers' badge shows a green fir tree suspended by a yellow parachute, with a white wing on either side. Different groups also wear their own badges. One example is the No Call Smoke Jumpers' badge, a circle surrounding an aircraft, with their name around the outside.

RAPPELLERS

Another group of airborne firefighters is the rappellers, who reach remote fires quickly by helicopter, then use ropes suspended from the helicopter to lower themselves to the ground. As this may entail drops of anything up to 300 feet (90 m), rappellers are trained to use a special body harness that fits around their waist and has two straps that pass between their legs, all of which clips together at the waist. This enables them to slide down the rope at a safe speed so that they do not break legs or ankles on landing. Like the smoke jumpers, they have heavy ankle boots for further protection.

They use the same special jump helmets and masks as smoke jumpers while making a landing, during which they carry a hard hat strapped to their legs—which they will wear while fighting the blaze—and a bag of small equipment strapped to their harness. Other heavier items of equipment, such as pumps, are lowered by rope from the helicopter. One obviously important piece of clothing for them is gloves, which must be tough and provide a good grip.

On the ground, rappellers wear the same basic uniform as the hotshots, fire-resistant coveralls in yellow or orange, or a windbreaker and trousers, and, of course, a hard hat.

These firefighters are wearing special protective overalls over their standard uniform to protect themselves and their uniforms from hazardous chemicals. Not even a small area of skin will be left exposed.

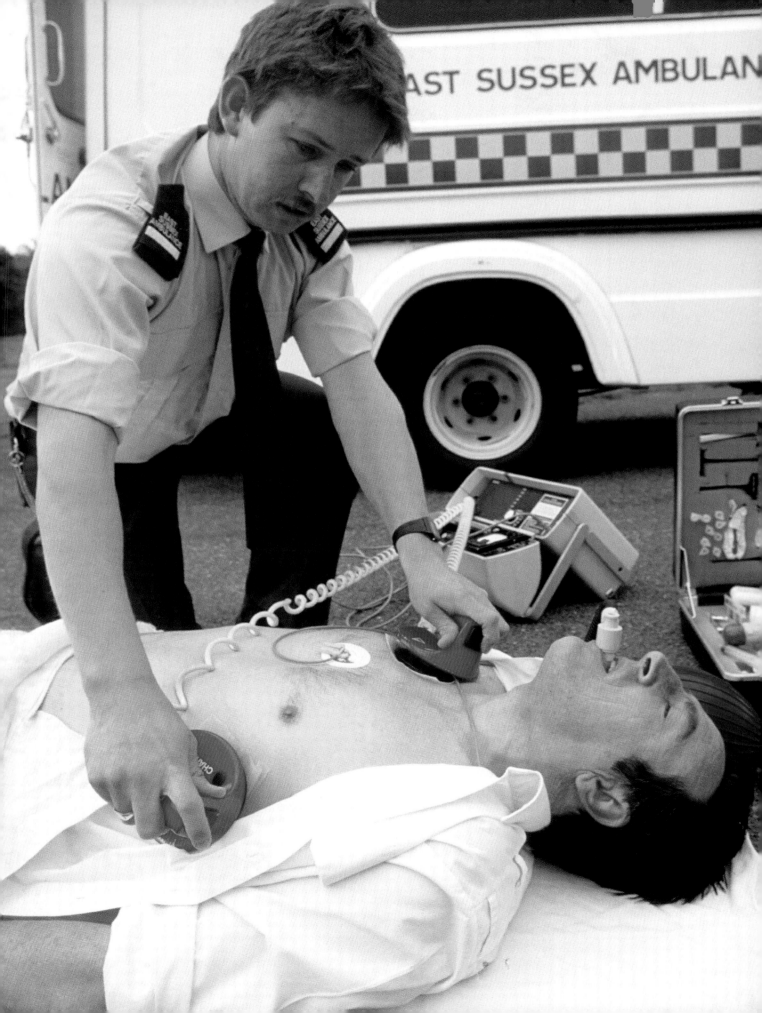

CHAPTER 2

Ambulance Services

Ambulance teams have come a long way since the days when they were merely expected to carry the sick or wounded on stretchers. Their roles, skills, and equipment have evolved, and their uniforms have kept pace with these changes to identify and protect the people serving in these jobs.

At the turn of the 20th century, most ambulances were horse-drawn wagons converted to carry patients on stretchers and to take injured or sick people to a hospital. With

The American ambulance driver (right) is wearing a shirt with a badge on the sleeve. The British paramedic (left) is wearing a standard uniform—a shirt with epaulets and tie.

the development of the gasoline engine, motorized vehicles gradually replaced horses. At this point, ambulance crews did nothing more than drive and carry stretchers. Early uniforms were often white to show that the wearer was part of a medical organization. Most wore white overalls, although some wore dark uniforms or no uniform at all.

U.S. VOLUNTEER AMBULANCES

At the beginning of World War I in 1914, the American Ambulance Hospital was established in a suburb of Paris to help care for the wounded soldiers of France. A dozen donated automobiles were hastily converted into ambulances. Driven by American volunteers, they shuttled between the frontline and the hospitals, carrying the wounded. Many more automobiles were donated, and more Americans volunteered to help with this work. Several members of the American Field Ambulance Service, as it was known, received bravery awards from France, including the Croix de Guerre.

N'envoyez pas trop de blessés de France. O mon doux Jesus, dans notre ambulance.

This World War I nurse is from a French field hospital. She is in the standard French nun's clothes of the time—most nurses were nuns who were trained to help the sick. Notice her Red Cross armband and the flag on the tent.

In France, most of the American ambulance volunteers soon took to wearing French military uniforms with Red Cross badges or the badge of the American Red Cross. The uniform was in a pale powder blue, known as horizon blue, and consisted of a long, four-pocket tunic with a shirt-type collar, baggy trousers wound tightly below the knee with **puttees**, and brown ankle boots. On the right arm, they wore a white armband bearing a red cross. The uniform was completed with a large, shirt-collared **greatcoat**, also in horizon blue, and a round, peaked cap called a kepi, such as French police wear, or a French helmet—which might have a red cross painted on the front.

American volunteer ambulances were again in action during the Spanish Civil War (1936–1939), during the Japanese invasion of China in the 1930s, and in Finland and France at the beginning of World War II (1939–1945). In Spain, where many of the U.S. volunteers were part of the Abraham Lincoln Battalion of the International Brigade, many took to wearing

THE ORIGIN OF AMBULANCE

The word *ambulance* comes from the Latin word *ambulare,* meaning "to walk"—which seems to be a contradiction, because an ambulance is a vehicle that carries the injured to a hospital. Originally, the word *ambulance* described hospitals, based in tents, that followed armies. Because these hospitals were not permanent, they were described as "ambulant," or moving. Later, the horse-drawn carts used for taking wounded soldiers from the frontline to the field hospitals became known as "ambulance wagons." By the mid-19th century, when the mobile hospitals were officially renamed field hospitals, the wagons became known simply as "ambulances." In 1863, two years into the American Civil War, they introduced special wagon trains called "ambulance trains" to carry the wounded to hospitals.

The men around this City of London Police motor ambulance in 1910 are wearing standard Metropolitan Police uniforms, except the driver, who has a Red Cross armband and gloves. The driver must have got cold and wet in the open cab.

the republican ambulance workers' outfit of short, black leather jacket, buff-colored riding **breeches**, long, lace-up boots or short boots with puttees or **gaiters**, and either a helmet marked with a red cross or the large Basque-style beret. Or they might wear the "mono" suit, an olive, double-breasted overall.

AMERICAN AMBULANCES BETWEEN THE WARS

Domestic ambulance drivers and attendants in the 1920s and 1930s were still little more than drivers and stretcher bearers. They were not expected to play any part in the medical treatment of casualties, although as the period went on, it became more common for them to receive some training in basic first aid.

Most ambulances were private or attached to a particular hospital, so there was a large range of uniforms. Most of them were like a white version of the police uniform: a double-breasted tunic, trousers, and a peaked cap bearing the name of the hospital. To modern eyes, they would look like ice-cream vendors.

AMERICAN VOLUNTEER AMBULANCES IN THE BLITZ

By the time of the London Blitz in 1940, there were numerous American volunteers—many of them women—working as ambulance crews in Britain.

Female members wore the military-style dress uniform of the American Red Cross: a long, waisted tunic with two pouch-pockets, knee-length skirt or trousers, and a soft peaked cap, all in **khaki**. The tunic was worn open-necked over a shirt and tie. Men also wore a long tunic with trousers and a peaked cap. For service wear, they wore khaki coveralls.

The American Red Cross cloth badge was worn on the tunic and coveralls, normally at the top of the arm. The badge consisted of a white circle containing a red cross in the center, with the words "AMERICAN RED CROSS" encircling it. The cap badge, which was also worn as a lapel badge, was of similar design in enameled metal, with the words in a blue band around the center.

BRITISH AMBULANCES IN WORLD WAR II

Air attacks on civilian populations were expected to create thousands of casualties. Such a situation would have completely swamped the existing ambulance provisions, so auxiliary or emergency ambulance groups were set up as an offshoot of the civil defense services.

In Britain, large cars and vans were converted into simple ambulances, while thousands of (mainly) women were trained as ambulance drivers and attendants. In order to set up this new service as quickly as possible, women who could already drive were preferred as potential drivers. In the late 1930s, there were far fewer automobiles on the road than there are today, and young women who could drive were almost entirely from well-off families, so the Civil Defence Auxiliary Ambulance Service was very much the province of "bright young things," as such girls were known (a decade or so earlier, they would have been called "flappers").

At first, ambulance crews had no uniforms as such: a **tommy** helmet (the nickname for a British Army tin helmet) with the letter "A" on the front, and perhaps an armband. However, by 1941, they were issued with the dark-blue Civil Defence uniform, ski cap, long, four-pocket tunic with "AMBULANCE" shoulder **flashes**, and ski pants.

THE POSTWAR PERIOD

Since the 19th century, it had been known that the sooner casualties received emergency medical treatment, the better their chances of survival. So during the 1950s and 1960s, drivers and attendants began to be trained in first aid, and ambulances carried more and more emergency medical equipment.

To reflect this changing function, the military-style uniform began to give way to a more practical form of dress. Ties and peaked caps disappeared, and tunics were replaced by shirts and jackets made of new manmade fabrics, which were more durable and easier to clean.

MODERN TRAINING AND UNIFORMS

Ambulance crews are now trained and equipped to make rapid diagnoses, supported by doctors and other specialists via the radio. They can staunch bleeding and apply splints and neck braces, and they are trained to deal with emergencies, such as heart attacks or brain hemorrhages. Of course, it is quite common for expectant mothers in labor to give birth in the ambulance on the way to the hospital, so ambulance crews have to be trained to deliver babies, too. Equipment routinely carried in an ambulance includes oxygen masks, saline drips, and **defibrillators**.

The training to administer emergency first aid takes a long time; one typical course for ambulance technicians lasts 16 months. A paramedic, trained to deal with more complex situations, takes at least another year to complete his or her training. This is all a long way from the first half of the 20th century, when all that was required of crews was that they lift the stretcher into the ambulance and drive it to the hospital.

Modern paramedics often wear a basic uniform of light blue or white short-sleeved shirt and dark blue or gray trousers with cargo pockets. The short sleeves are for hygiene, like operating-room gowns (long sleeves might accidentally brush against wounds, causing infection). Over this, they wear

Today, Red Cross workers can be found working almost anywhere around the world, often helping during natural and ecological distasters. This worker is in a remote part of Africa and uses a radio to communicate with a Red Cross base.

high-visibility jackets; a common color is red. Alternative outer clothing for ambulance crews includes zipper-fronted coveralls, with long or short sleeves, in a wide range of colors.

Many of these outer garments are brightly colored, although some crews wear a reflective vest over the top of the coveralls, again for high visibility. It is often their job to pick up people from fire scenes or at night, where smoke or darkness limits their ability to be seen. Added to this are the risks of working in dangerous locations—such as car crashes on freeways, where other vehicles are driving past, often at great speed—which is why ambulance crews need to be easily spotted from a distance.

Visibility is enhanced by pieces of reflective material that are sewn onto the uniform—patches, dots, or badges. Often, rescue-service clothing has reflective strips around the sleeves, body, and legs.

Hard Hats

For rescues in dangerous conditions, ambulance crews and paramedics are issued hard hats, usually in white. Many of these bear an organization shield or logo on the front and the wearer's function in a crescent around it. One badge retailer has over 20 medical variations on its list, including ambulance, paramedic, ambulance captain, ambulance chief, and cardiac rescue tech.

Other Insignia

Many medical personnel wear embroidered cloth badges featuring a symbol called the star of life. This is in the form of a six-pointed asterisk, like a capital letter "X" with a vertical band going through it—the vertical band being a caduceus, the medical symbol of a staff with a snake wrapped around it. Probably the simplest example of this is a badge made up of a blue star of life set in a white circle. Other badges feature the star of life and information that identifies the wearer's specialty. One example is a white circle 3 inches (9 cm) in diameter with a blue border, the words "EMERGENCY MEDICAL TECHNICIAN" going around the outside, and a blue star of life inside with white staff and snake. Of course, the badges come in many shapes besides circles; one example is a white shield with a blue border, blue star of life, and the title "EMERGENCY MEDICAL TEAM" above. A further variation is in the form of a white **lozenge** with a blue border, blue star of life in the center, the word "EMERGENCY" in red above, and the words "AMBULANCE SERVICE" below in blue.

Other cloth badges are in the form of imitation gold or silver shields, such as the police use, bearing such lettering as "EMERGENCY MEDICAL

These ambulance crews are on standby during a mountain rescue emergency.
Note the crosses on the backs of their jackets and the bright orange color and
reflective strips for high visibility.

TECHNICIAN" or "EMERGENCY MEDICAL SERVICES." Like the other badges, these are worn in several places on coats and shirts—on the upper or lower arm, on or above the breast pocket, and on the cap.

Some badges denote that the wearer is qualified to carry out cardiopulmonary resuscitation (CPR), which means that the person can attempt to revive someone whose heart has stopped or who has stopped breathing. One example of such a badge is a red heart inside a white shield with red border, above which are the letters "CPR" in blue and, going through the heart, a blue zigzag line, like the display on a heart monitor.

There are also badges that identify the town, hospital, or organization to which the wearer belongs. These may be separate or included in the specialist badge.

AIR AMBULANCES

In some parts of the world, men—or mules, steer, reindeer, and other animals—are used to pull ambulance carts, but in such countries as the U.S., where transportation systems are well developed, the automobile is the main form of ambulance, although ambulance trains and air ambulances are also used.

During the Korean War, helicopters were used with stretchers strapped precariously to the sides—outside—which can be seen in old episodes of the television series *M*A*S*H*. The first civilian air ambulance flight was in October 1973, from Missouri to Texas in a single-engine aircraft, with a pilot accompanied by an emergency medical technician. The copilot's seat was removed to make room for an ordinary ambulance stretcher to be belted to the floor. All the medical equipment normally carried in a ground ambulance was also placed in the aircraft. Today, air ambulances are equipped like a mini hospital-emergency department.

The paramedics or medical technicians working in air ambulances wear exactly the same uniforms as ordinary paramedics, but often with badges that distinguish them as air ambulance workers.

BIKE SQUADS

In a further attempt to speed up response times, several emergency medical agencies have recently started to organize and deploy paramedics on bicycles at major public events. This is because crowds can limit the access and response time of normal ambulance vehicles. Recently, this service has spread to congested inner cities, where gridlocked streets can stop emergency medical aid from getting through in larger vehicles.

Bike-squad paramedics wear a uniform that is a cross between a normal paramedic uniform and a cycling outfit. This consists of cycling shorts and helmet, with the paramedic's short-sleeved shirt under a reflective vest, a belt, and a small backpack containing emergency equipment, along with the service's own badges.

The driver of this motorcycle is a member of an ambulance service and is trained to administer emergency first aid. The motorcycle has compartments to carry medical equipment and can get through traffic faster than an ambulance.

CHAPTER 3

Civil Defense

It was civilians' sense of vulnerability to enemy attack on home ground that led to an official, coordinated response to such things as air raids or nuclear attack. Civil defense has since evolved to deal with natural disasters, too, and the uniforms reflect the need to be identifiable in an emergency.

AMERICAN CIVIL DEFENSE DURING WORLD WAR II

In December 1941, the Japanese launched a massive air attack on Pearl Harbor in Hawaii, dragging the U.S. into the Second World War, which had been raging for two years in Europe. President Franklin D. Roosevelt declared the United States in "a state

This British female air raid warden (left) is in civilian clothes, apart from the helmet. Uniforms were not issued until 1940; these were oilskin suits, with gas masks (right).

of unlimited emergency," and each city was made responsible for recruiting and organizing its own civil-defense organization. Generally, the system that arose was modeled on the one the British had developed "under fire."

The sheer number of volunteers involved were huge. The *San Francisco News* of August 9, 1941, reported that in California alone "a volunteer aircraft-warning program will require 20,000 civilian volunteers manning 1,664 observation posts throughout the state." The sheer size of the operation meant that a uniform was rarely issued. Also, as each community was responsible for setting up its own organization, it would also be responsible for providing a uniform, and few could afford it. Most followed the early British example and made use of helmets, armbands, and service badges. The messenger service badge, for example, was a bolt of lightning; bomb-squad badges had an aircraft as viewed from above; and rescue workers' badges had a ladder logo. Those state, town, and other officials whose task was to control the local civil defense had badges with a small, five-pointed star over the letters "CDC" (Civil Defense Control).

Early armbands were quite individual; most merely displayed the name of the wearer's service—"RESCUE," "BLOCK WARDEN," and so on. In 1942, Charles Coiner designed a range of service badges. All of them were set inside a white equilateral triangle, which was itself set into a royal blue circle. Inside the triangle was a red logo, and each of the various civil defense services had its own logo. This badge was used on enameled lapel badges, embroidered badges, armbands, helmets, and documents.

The civil defense helmet was a round, domed affair with a rim, or a World War I U.S. Army helmet. They were usually painted white for increased visibility in a blackout and often bore Charles Coiner's service badge on the front, sometimes with other information, such as the name of a city. Later, armbands were either a long white band or a square of white cloth attached to two strips of elastic with the Coiner service logo on them.

Air Raid Wardens

Just as in Britain, the central local personnel of the civil defense services were the air raid wardens. They had many tasks, which included checking that everyone carried out the strict blackout rules, such as stopping any light from escaping from a house. In a raid, they had to help fight fires; direct people caught in the street to shelters; report any fires, fallen bombs, or the presence of gas; administer elementary first aid; and assist victims in damaged buildings. They were often seen as busybodies or figures of fun, as is shown by the 1943 film *Air Raid Wardens,* starring Laurel and Hardy.

The warden's badge had the white triangle divided into a series of seven red and white diagonal stripes. These were on armbands, painted on the front of helmets, and available as enameled metal badges. In some areas, coveralls were issued, and an embroidered version of the badge was worn on the chest or sleeve. Other local variations included a side cap, similar to

Laurel and Hardy in the 1943 movie, *Air Raid Wardens* wear the wardens' logo on their white, 1917 U.S. Army helmets. Their armbands (which would have the same badge), their gas mask bags, and their whistles on lanyards are all standard issue.

DEALING WITH DISASTER

In the 1930s, people became obsessed with the idea that a future war would be the end of civilization. This was graphically demonstrated in the 1938 movie *Things to Come,* based on a novel by H.G. Wells. The movie shows a war being declared, and immediately, the sky is full of bombers dropping high-explosive and gas bombs; within seconds, the streets are littered with piles of dead bodies and rubble. It was this fear that led to the setting up of British Civil Defence to try to deal with just such a scenario.

those worn by Boy Scouts, with a small version of the embroidered service badge sewn onto it.

The Medical Corps

Air raids created a vast need for emergency medical aid. Sometimes, trained doctors would provide this, but trained first-aiders could give much of it. Together, they made up the Civil Defense Medical Corps. Civil Defense doctors' and nurses' badges contained a red, winged staff, such as is often seen in the star-of-life emblem, while first-aiders had a red cross. Many carried a bag, often marked with a red cross, that contained equipment, bandages, and so on.

Fire Services

There were two main fire services: the fire watchers, whose job was to look out for fires started by incendiary bombs from their posts on factory roofs, etc., and the ordinary firefighters, including the auxiliary firefighters, who were volunteers trained to help the "regulars."

The fire watchers' logo was a red, three-pointed flame. Auxiliary firefighters had a red Maltese cross in the white triangle as their logo, often on a Civil

Defense helmet painted red. Sometimes, they were issued a fire department uniform; regular fire officers, who wore special badges on their ordinary uniform to show this, often commanded them.

Auxiliary Police

Regular officers also commanded auxiliary policemen, whose badge was a red shield in the white triangle. Some were issued a police uniform. As with the firefighters, regular police who worked as part of the civil defense structure were issued special badges to wear on their uniforms. One example of this is a pair of collar badges, screw-backed metal badges showing a crossed rifle and police baton with a U.S. Army helmet in the center bearing the letters "CD." A variation on this, for an emergency ambulance crew, has a large letter "A" on top of the helmet.

The regular police sometimes controlled much of the local civil defense organization and this is shown on the badges or helmets; examples of this include a helmet with a warden badge above the words "L.A. POLICE," and similar marking on a fire-watcher helmet. Other variations indicate rank, such as a civil defense helmet bearing the auxiliary police badge above the words "2ND LIEUT."

BRITISH CIVIL DEFENCE DURING WORLD WAR II

In Britain, the term civil defence began to be used in the late 1930s to cover a group of services whose task was either wholly or mainly to deal with the growing threat of air raids. Civil Defence was made up of several parts—the police, the fire brigades, and a group called the "ARP" (Air Raid Precautions).

Germany's Blitz on Britain—by bombers and V1 and V2 rocket attacks—lasted from early 1940 until March 1945, during which time 2,379 Civil Defence workers were killed in the line of duty and 4,459 seriously injured.

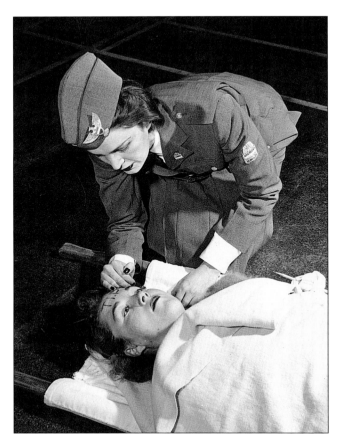

A member of the American Women's Voluntary Service, this volunteer nurse has the AWVS shoulder and lapel badges and the cap badge. The writing on the patient's forehead is a record of emergency treatment given, such as any drugs administered.

At first, it was felt that, to emphasize their civilian status, Civil Defence workers should not wear uniforms; instead, they were issued armbands and lapel badges. The armbands might be marked "ARP" or "CIVIL DEFENCE," or might show the wearer's job, such as "MESSENGER" or "CONTROLLER," or give a local area, such as "CROYDON RESCUE."

Late in 1939, however, a simple uniform was produced. This early uniform took the form of coveralls for men and raincoats for women, both in dark-blue denim, with a red embroidered badge reading "ARP." These were worn with a tommy helmet with a letter on the front to show their job—"W" for air raid warden, "R" for rescue worker, "A" for ambulance worker, and so on. Ordinary members of the ARP had a black helmet with white lettering, while officers wore white helmets with black lettering for easy recognition in the blacked-out streets.

In 1941, a heavy battle-dress uniform in dark blue **serge** replaced these lightweight uniforms. This was made up of a short blouson jacket, trousers, greatcoat, and beret for men, and a longer, waisted jacket, greatcoat, skirt or trousers, and ski cap or felt hat for women. The badge had now changed to a yellow "CD" surmounted by a crown, worn on the left breast pocket of the tunic; a smaller version was worn on the cap. Other badges, for rank and specialty, were also in yellow.

After the war, Civil Defence had a new job—to prepare for a possible nuclear war. Despite its changed role, the basic Civil Defence uniform stayed the same, although the badge was revised, being now a heraldic lion with the words "CIVIL DEFENCE CORPS" around it, surmounted by a crown.

CIVIL DEFENSE IN THE 1950s AND 1960S

Soon after World War II, a new kind of international conflict developed—the Cold War. The Civil Defense Corps was given a new, or rather altered, role. Now, the training focused on preparing for a nuclear war.

Civil Defense became a more unified body, and the different badges gave way to a single badge of the same design bearing the red letters "CD," shaped to form a circle. This logo was used on armbands and on metal and embroidered badges; one embroidered badge, for example, had "CD" in the triangle and circle, with "POLICE" above and "WEST VIRGINIA" below, in red. During this time, the steel helmet was replaced by a fiberglass version, which was of a similar shape, but with three parallel ridges on the crown for added strength. An alternative was the plastic liner of the M41 U.S. military helmet, painted white.

CIVIL DEFENSE TODAY

Today, the job of civil defense has grown immensely. They still train for enemy attacks on the country, but the range of response has been enlarged to include nuclear, biological, and chemical warfare, plus cyberterrorism. Furthermore, the job of the Civil Defense Corps has expanded to deal with natural environmental and ecological threats and disasters, such as earthquakes, as well as large-scale accidents.

CHAPTER 4

Search and Rescue

With amazing regularity, and sometimes an alarming lack of common sense, people get themselves into difficulties that require the intervention of professional rescuers—and the rescuers count on their protective clothing and specialized equipment.

This category of rescue services contains a whole range of different groups whose main tasks are twofold, as the name suggests: first, to find lost people, and then to render assistance or deliver them

A rescue swimmer (left) will dive from a helicopter into the sea to help anyone in difficulties. Mountain rescue workers (right) have to work in extreme conditions.

to the nearest hospital. The main groups involved are the Coast Guard, mountain rescue, and forest rangers, but there are others, including dive groups (which perform underwater search-and-rescue operations) and lifeguards.

This lifeguard, at a lifeguard station in New Jersey, is wearing a high-visibility red top as part of his uniform. The float below him and the whistle on the lanyard around his neck are part of his equipment.

U.S. LIFE-SAVING SERVICE

Federal responsibility for search and rescue began in 1831, when seven **cutters** were ordered to patrol the coast in search of persons in distress. Soon after, special lifesaving stations were built on the New Jersey and Long Island coasts, equipped with an iron boat on a wagon and lifesaving equipment.

The U.S. Life-Saving Service was founded in 1878 under the Treasury Department, and eventually, it had lifesaving stations on all the coasts of the United States. Each station was in the charge of a keeper, under whom were the "surfmen," as his men were called. The number of surfmen posted at each station was the number needed to man the largest boat there, which was usually 10.

Life-Saving station personnel were not authorized to wear uniforms until 1889. Once

ON GUARD

Most large beach resorts and pools have their own lifeguards, who, like other members of the rescue services, are trained in first aid and especially in artificial respiration—or, as it is more often called today, resuscitation. Lifeguards usually wear swimsuits in bright colors, like orange or yellow, with a t-shirt printed with "BEACH PATROL" or "LIFEGUARD" across the chest, and sometimes the name of the town or pool. Perhaps the most famous lifeguard of the 20th century was a young man—later to be a movie star and eventually a politician—by the name of Ronald Reagan, 40th president of the United States.

uniforms were authorized, there was a stiff protest because personnel had to pay for the uniforms themselves. The uniforms for the Life-Saving Service were set out in the regulations of 1899. There were only two varieties, corresponding to the two uniformed ranks in the service—keepers and surfmen—who were directed to "wear their uniforms at all times when on duty."

Keepers' Uniforms

The keeper's uniform was of dark indigo-blue **kersey** or flannel. The double-breasted coat was thigh-length, with two rows of five **gilt** buttons and a rolling collar. There were two outside pockets at the hips, and two small regulation buttons on each cuff. With this was worn a seven-button collarless vest and trousers "cut in the prevailing style," both in the same material as the coat. The regulations were strict; one example stated that "trousers rolled up or tucked into boots other than hip rubber boots is positively forbidden." The buttons on this and other items of uniform were to bear the service device, a life buoy crossed by an oar and a boat hook.

For heavy weather, a double-breasted, navy blue, pea jacket-style overcoat was authorized. Like the coat, there were two rows of five gilt buttons, and like most seamen's coats, it was short. The bottom edge was to reach the tips of a man's fingers when his arms hung by his sides; a long overcoat, when wet (and sailor's coats are often soaking wet), is uncomfortable and awkward to wear. Regulations were equally strict with regards to another aspect: "The overcoat will be worn completely buttoned."

On top of this was worn a dark-blue peaked cap, the peak being of black patent leather. On the band around the cap, the service emblem of life buoy, boat hook, and oar was embroidered in gold, with the letters "U.S." above and "LSS" below, also in gold.

In stormy weather, keepers might wear a storm suit, like the one worn by surfmen, and a type of storm hat, described as a sou'wester or southwester. The latter was painted black, with the service device, like that on the cap, painted on the front.

Surfmen's Uniforms

The surfmen wore a coat similar to the keeper's, but single-breasted and with four plain, black buttons. Like the keeper's coat, it had a rolling collar that could be turned up and buttoned to give protection against the wind and rain. A pleat two inches (5 cm) wide ran from each shoulder downward on front and back; a belt, in the same material as the coat, passed through the four pleats. The service badge was worn on the upper-right sleeve, while on the left was the individual's seniority number embroidered in white silk or linen—the most senior surfman being number "1."

The overcoat and trousers were the same as the keeper's, although, like the coat, plain, black buttons were to be worn on the overcoat. The cap, too, was similar to the one issued to keepers, but instead of the service device, there was "U.S. LIFE-SAVING SERVICE" on the band in gold. For summer wear, a white linen version could be used. They might also wear a black-painted sou'wester like the keepers, although on the front they had to have the station name and the letters "LSS." They could also wear a canvas hat with a large quilted brim, like the sou'wester. All personnel could, if they wished, wear a storm suit, a coat, and trousers made of brown rubber cloth or cotton **duck**

WARTIME FUNCTIONS OF THE COAST GUARD

Even during wartime, when the Coast Guard becomes part of the armed services, it still continues to carry out lifesaving missions. During World War II, Coast Guard cutters carried out search-and-rescue patrols for airmen who had been shot down in the sea or sailors whose ships had been sunk; Coast Guard aircraft and cutters patrolled for enemy submarines in U.S. waters and rescued more than 1,500 survivors of torpedo attacks. Later, during the Vietnam War, Coast Guard pilots flew combat search-and-rescue missions over hostile territory, locating and picking up shot-down air crews. Today, members of the Coast Guard may use riot-control gear to help at times of civil unrest.

treated with linseed oil, with the name of the station painted in black on the breast. Alternatively, overalls of unbleached cotton duck were allowed, which were to have a large pocket on the right leg, with two buttons on the flap— what we would call a cargo pocket.

THE COAST GUARD

On May 26, 1913, the U.S. Life-Saving Service and the Revenue Cutter Service were combined to create the United States Coast Guard, which was to come under the direction of the U.S. Navy in wartime and the Treasury Department during times of peace. At this point, the uniforms of the Life-Saving Service and the Revenue Cutter Service were scrapped, and a common Coast Guard uniform was produced.

One of the Coast Guard's oldest jobs comprises what are known as search-and-rescue missions (SAR). "Minimizing loss of life, injury, and property damage by giving aid to people in distress at sea" has always been one of the Coast Guard's priorities. The U.S. Coast Guard conducts, on average, six search-and-rescue missions every day, using boats, cutters, and helicopters, either individually or in combination.

The first Coast Guard uniform was a double-breasted, dark-blue service coat similar to that worn by the U.S. Navy, although without epaulets. Because of this, rank badges were worn on the lower sleeve, with the Coast Guard badge—the shield of the Treasury Department on an anchor— above the rank stripes. Men below the rank of petty officer adopted the Navy-style white duck hat, although the traditional flat cap remained standard. The vessel name on the hat ribbon was that of the Coast Guard ship, plus the letters "CG." Coast Guard officers wore a Navy-style peaked cap. Their cap badges consisted of a large spread eagle and shield, with the eagle holding a horizontal anchor in its talons. Other ranks' cap badges consisted of a pair of crossed anchors, surmounted by a circle in which was

This U.S. Coast Guard member is in the new lighter blue uniform. Notice the USCG badges on his cap and chest and the Coast Guard emblem—a pair of anchors surmounted by the Treasury shield—in white on the vest.

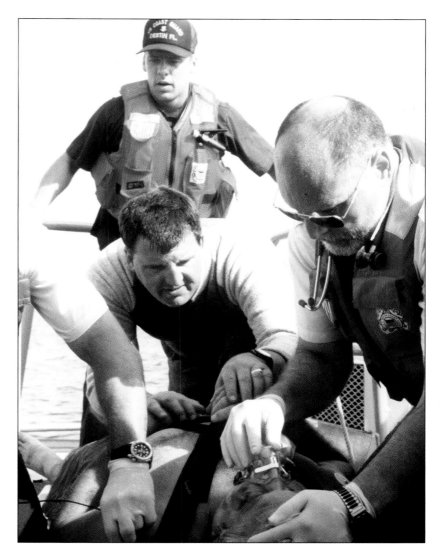

the shield, with the words "UNITED STATES COAST GUARD 1790" around the outside.

Coast Guard Aircraft

In the 20th century, the Coast Guard expanded its field of operations from the water to the air when, in 1920, it first made use of a borrowed Navy biplane, a practice that was to become commonplace by the 1930s, especially for search-and-rescue missions.

For ranks above petty officer, working dress for Coast Guard aviators was in forest-green **gabardine** or serge for winter, and khaki cotton, or chino, for summer. The jacket was a single-breasted, four flap-pocket tunic with built-in belt. Green epaulets with black rank markings and Coast Guard shields were

These members of the RNLI (the Royal National Lifeboat Institute) are in the British version of the Life-Saving Service uniform. They are wearing standard high-visibility waterproof jackets and life jackets over their uniforms.

worn on the winter jacket. Under the jacket, a khaki shirt was worn with a black tie. Finally, a folding flying cap was issued, edged in black and gold.

Coast Guard aviators had their own special badge—the Coast Guard fouled anchor and shield, with wings—which was worn on the left breast of the jacket, like aviators' wings. Air crew had similar wings with, in the center, the letters "A" and "C" on either side of an anchor, all within a circle.

World War II Uniforms

In 1941, the Coast Guard went to war along with the rest of the United States, coming under the control of the Navy Department. Uniforms became officially a modification of Navy dress, in that the clothes were the same as naval uniforms: a blue winter dress-uniform for both officers and men, khaki **undress** combination with sewn-in belt, and white summer dress-uniform. Officers wore the combination cap, a peaked cap with interchangeable covers in white, khaki, and blue. Their main distinguishing mark was the Coast Guard shield, which continued to be worn above the rank badges or, in the case of women, on the lapels. Other Coast Guard insignia included their buttons—an anchor with a rope border—aviators' wings, officers' cap badges, and so on.

The only exception to this similarity of Navy and Coast Guard uniforms was the substitution of olive drab for the white service uniform for warrant-officer keepers of lifesaving stations. The buttons on this were dull-finish bronze. Surfmen had an olive-drab, cotton duck summer uniform, also with bronze buttons. **Chevrons** and specialty marks were in blue. The specialty mark retained a variation of the old service's ring buoy device—with two crossed oars instead of the boat hook and oar combination.

This unity of Coast Guard and Navy uniforms continued until after the war, when the Coast Guard was transferred back to the Department of Transportation.

Women in the Coast Guard

In November 1942, a new branch of the U.S. Coast Guard was set up—the Coast Guard Women's Reserve, better known as the SPARS. It was disbanded at the end of the war, but was soon re-formed.

The SPARS uniform consisted of a navy-blue skirt of serge, gabardine, or tropical **worsted** and a four-button blouse with rounded lapels, with the Coast Guard shield worn on the sleeve. As with uniforms today, rating badges and rank stripes were worn on the sleeves. One big difference was in the officers' uniforms—rank stripes on their whites were blue instead of gold; this denoted reserve ranks. The SPARS had a variety of shirts, including work shirts, silk dress shirts, and everyday cotton versions. They also came in several colors, depending on the occasion and the wearer's rank.

Enlisted women wore a round-crowned, snap-brimmed hat that had "U.S. COAST GUARD" in gold letters across the hat band. The officers' hat, often referred to as a boat, bore the same cap device that male officers wore. However, no provisions were made for women with the rank of commander or above to wear reserve blue **scrambled eggs** on the brim. For informal use, both officers and enlisted women wore **garrison** caps.

During the summer, SPARS' workwear included a gray-and-white striped,

These members of SPARS are wearing a variety of uniform styles. One woman (far left) has rank stripes near the bottom edge of the sleeves on her jacket. Note the different styles of hats.

short-sleeved **seersucker** dress with a removable jacket. For summer dress occasions, another version of the standard uniform was made in a white fabric. Women's winter uniforms were dark blue.

Rescue Swimmers

A recent development in Coast Guard rescues has been the introduction of rescue swimmers. These are specialists who jump from the helicopter into the sea to aid people in distress. Since 1991, all Coast Guard air stations have had a rescue swimmer stationed there.

Rescue swimmers wear the ordinary Coast Guard uniform, but with special wings. This badge takes the form of a winged circle, inside of which is the "star of life," under a pair of crossed flippers. For rescues, swimmers wear red wet suits (either full-body or with short legs and arms), goggles, and flippers.

A Change of Color

Recently, a new, lighter blue, single-breasted uniform has been introduced. The particular shade of blue was chosen because it was different from those used by the other services. The only uniforms still shared with the Navy today are the officers' white summer-service dress and full-dress combinations.

MOUNTAIN RESCUE

Today, mountain climbing is such a popular, established pastime that it is hard to realize that a few centuries ago, no one would have dreamed of climbing a mountain for fun. As the mountains became an increasingly popular vacation destination, it was seen that providing an official mountain rescue team was important, and local teams began to be set up. At first, these were groups of local guides gathered together at short notice. Later, as rescue techniques and equipment became more specialized, key team members were employed full-time and were extensively trained. Training now involves

These Coast Guards are part of an ice rescue team. Clothes that keep the wearer warm and dry even when he or she is submerged in icy water are vital. This team is performing a training exercise rather than an actual rescue.

emergency first-aid techniques, including dealing with **hypothermia**, a common problem at high altitudes.

As for all rescue personnel, mountain rescue clothing and equipment have been very much affected by high technology. Clothing is made of lightweight, stormproof material in high-visibility colors. Many climbers wear lightweight jackets called anoraks, made from nylon or some other waterproof material. Trousers are of a strong yet flexible material, stitched with tough thread. Often, they are reinforced at critical areas, such as the knees. For rescues in extremely bad weather, a coverall in something like silicone-impregnated nylon might be used. Like the anorak, this is fastened by either Velcro or a heavyweight zipper, probably in nylon.

Two of the most important items of dress are the helmet and gloves. Gloves are often of cowhide or goatskin, or have flexible rubber palm and finger pieces that are specially contoured for maximum grip. Helmets need to be lightweight but tough, and as such, they usually have a shell made of Kevlar or thermo-formed ABS, or some other modern fiber. They have strong chin straps and polyfoam lining pads for shock absorption.

As the temperature can drop rapidly at high elevations, mountain rescue workers carry spare clothes in their backpacks, along with equipment. This includes obvious items, such as map and compass, first-aid kit, pocket knife, and backpack; climbing equipment, such as helmet, ice ax, ice hammer, and crampons; equipment for the unexpected, such as an emergency storm shelter, tent, and sleeping bag; a three-day supply of food, stove, fuel, and cooking pot; and other items, such as waterproof notebook and pen, whistle, headlight with extra bulb, extra batteries, and two water bottles. It is amazing how many rescue calls are caused by people who have undertaken a climb without even the most basic equipment.

Mountain rescue teams wear the Mountain Rescue badge, a circular badge showing a blue mountain peak with a white cross on it, surrounded by the

This mountain rescue incident in the U.S. shows a range of rescue organizations: the fire department, a police helicopter, and members of a mountain rescue team. Many such rescues involve several agencies.

words "MOUNTAIN RESCUE" in blue on a white background. Local teams have their own badges, such as the Grand County Mountain Rescue team, whose members wear a yellow shield with a cross in the middle showing a snowcapped mountain range crossed by an ice ax, with the words "GRAND COUNTY" above and "SEARCH AND RESCUE" below.

CAVE RESCUE

Cave exploring has become increasingly more popular, and as a result, cave rescue teams have been formed. These teams wear outfits similar to mountain rescue teams, although their helmets are slightly different—they have fittings for a headlight, and their clothing and gloves need to be far more waterproof.

FOREST AND PARK RANGERS

America's national parks have existed since the 19th century, providing the public with a chance to enjoy the open-air life. In 1916, the National Parks Service was set up to administer the 38 national parks, and the system included rangers to patrol them. As part of their job, forest and park rangers are trained to carry out what is called "wilderness search-and-rescue" missions to find hikers, campers, and others lost or injured in the forest.

Rangers' uniforms were originally based on Army uniforms—a long, four-pocket tunic, shirt, tie, and riding breeches, with a "lemon-squeezer" campaign hat, like the one Canadian Mounties still wear. Now, their day-to-day uniform is less rigid, with shirt and pants in chino or Forest Service spruce green, which can be worn with a windbreaker-type short jacket and baseball-type cap. Badges are local, and the National Park Service shield is in brown, showing a green tree and white buffalo on a green foreground, with a distant snowcapped mountain range and, in the top right, the words "NATIONAL PARKS SERVICE."

Dress uniform is similar to the old uniform, although usually with straight trousers instead of breeches.

CLOTHES THAT WORK

The dress of rescue workers has changed—in many ways quite dramatically—over the last century. For the most part, this has been driven by their changing roles and by rapidly improving technology. New equipment and techniques have meant that rescue teams have become specialists whose clothes reflect the unique jobs they do.

The realization that speed is of the essence if the injured are to recover has led to first aid and emergency medical training becoming widespread. Insignia on uniforms indicate the wearer's ability to perform such treatment, as well as other functions, rank, local area, and so on.

From uniforms that were mostly ceremonial, to functional emergency wear, we have charted not only their dress, but also the emergence of new groups, as new inventions of the last century, such as aircraft, have created new dangers and new types of rescue. It has been an evolution that will continue to unfold, as new technologies and new dangers are presented to us.

A Forest Ranger from Finger Lakes National Park, New York, is in his everyday service uniform of shirt and cap. Notice the U.S. Forest Service badges on his shoulder, chest, and cap.

GLOSSARY

Air pack helmet with oxygen mask that enables firefighters to work in the smoke and fumes created by fire

Blouson jacket a waist-length jacket, usually gathered at the waist

Breeches short pants covering the hips and thighs and fitting snugly at the lower edges at or just below the knee

Chevrons V-shaped stripes worn on uniforms to show rank, such as sergeant

Cutter a single-masted, fore and aft-rigged sailing boat

Defibrillator a device that applies an electric shock to a fibrillating heart (one that is contracting quickly and irregularly) in order to reestablish rhythmic beating

Duck (n.): a durable, closely woven, usually cotton fabric

Epaulet a flap of cloth from the shoulder to the neck on which rank and other badges are fixed

Flash British military term meaning a colored piece of cloth (or tassle) that is a distinguishing emblem

Gabardine a firm, hard-finished, durable fabric twilled with diagonal ribs on the right side

Gaiters a cloth or leather leg covering reaching from the instep to above the ankle or to mid-calf or knee

Garrison a permanent military installation

Gilt overlaid with a thin covering of gold

Greatcoat a heavy overcoat

Hypothermia subnormal temperature of the body

Kersey a thick, heavy, cotton-and-wool twill fabric

Khaki dull brown-green color

Lozenge a figure with four equal sides and two acute and two obtuse angles, similar to a diamond

Maltese cross a cross that resembles the cross form, but has the outer face of each arm indented in a V

Piping a trim of contrasting material sewn in the seams or around the edges of a garment

Puttee a strip of material wound around the lower leg to hold trousers tight

Scrambled eggs military slang for the decoration on senior officers' cap peaks

Seersucker: a light fabric of linen, cotton, or rayon usually striped and slightly puckered

Serge a durable twilled fabric having a smooth clear face and a pronouned diagonal rib on the front and the back

Star of life medical symbol in the form of an

asterisk, bearing a staff with a snake wrapped around it

Tommy a British soldier

Tunic a simple slip-on garment made with or without sleeves and usually knee-length or longer, belted at the waist

Undress informal dress

Waders thigh-length rubber boots

Walkie-talkie a small, easily carried, two-way radio set

Welt a double edge, strip, insert, or seam for ornament or reinforcement

Worsted a smooth compact yarn from long wool fibers

TIMELINE

1735: Benjamin Franklin sets up America's first volunteer fire department in Philadelphia.

1765: George Washington introduces the first fire engine to America.

1861–1865: The American Civil War.

1863: Ambulance trains are introduced to carry Civil War wounded.

1871: The Great Chicago Fire.

1906: The Great San Francisco Earthquake and Fire.

1913: The Life-Saving Service and the Revenue Cutter Service combine to create the U.S. Coast Guard.

1914: The start of World War I; the American Ambulance Hospital is set up in Paris.

1916: The National Parks Service is founded in the U.S.

1918: The first firefighting departments are formed in the U.S; the first aircraft are used to spot forest fires.

1920: The first use of aircraft by the Coast Guard.

1936–1939: The Spanish Civil War.

1940: The first operational use of smoke jumpers.

1940–1945: The German Blitz on Britain.

1941: The Japanese attack on Pearl Harbor; the Coast Guard becomes temporarily part of the U.S. Navy, adopting their uniforms.

1942: The U.S. Coast Guard Women's Reserve (SPARs) is founded.

1950–1953: The Korean War.

1965–1975: The Vietnam War.

1973: The first civilian air-ambulance flight.

1991: Rescue swimmers are stationed in all Coast Guard air stations.

FURTHER INFORMATION

BOOKS

Maniscalco, Paul M. *When Violence Erupts: A Survival Guide for Emergency Responders.* American Academy of Orthopaedic Surgeons. Sudbury: Jones and Bartlett, 2002.

Picciotto, Richard. *Last Man Down: A New York City Fire Chief and the Collapse of the World Trade Center.* New York: Penguin Putnam, 2002.

Post, Carl J. *Omaha Orange: A Popular History of EMS in America.* Sudbury: Jones and Bartlett, 2001.

Ray, Slim. *Swiftwater Rescue.* Asheville: CFS Press, 1996.

Sargent, Chase. *Confined Space Rescue.* Saddle Brook, N.J.: Fire Engineering Book Department, 2000.

Vines, Tom and Steve Hudson. *High-Angle Rescue Techniques.* St. Louis: Mosby, 1999.

Walton, S. C. *First-Response Guide to Street Drugs.* Boston: Quinlan Publishing, 2001.

ONLINE SOURCES

Boulder Rural Fire Department
http://www.brfd.boulder.co.us/index2.html
Boulder Rural Fire Department's official site with news, information, and tips on fire safety. Also carries details of opportunites to volunteer.

Houston Fire Musem
www.houstonfiremuseum.org
Interactive Web site for the Texas-based museum, which covers the history of firefighting in Houston and educates the community on fire safety.

Welcome to Safety Campus

www.safetycampus.com

Site offering online, interactive training and community courses in CPR and other first-aid measures, teaching appropriate action in emergency situations.

www.uscg.mil/hq/g-cp/history/collect.html

The historian's office pages from the official Web site of the U.S. Coast Guard. Masses of information (for example, on uniforms, events, and various types of craft used by the Coast Guard); also major sections on such diverse areas as search and rescue, maritime safety, law enforcement, and the International Ice Patrol.

ABOUT THE AUTHORS

Mike Brown lives in London, England, where he writes part-time and teaches part-time, in addition to giving talks and lectures on 20th-century history and architecture to a wide range of audiences, from primary schools to retirement groups. He has written a book on Britain's Civil Defence Services in World War II, *Put That Light Out,* published in 2000. Other books include *A Child's War,* and, in conjunction with his wife, Carol Harris, *The Wartime House.*

Carol Harris is a freelance journalist and lecturer specializing in the 1920s, 1930s, and 1940s. Carol's first book was *Collecting Twentieth-Century Fashion and Accessories* (Mitchell Beazley 1999) followed by the pamphlet, *Putting on the Ritz—Women and the Styles of the 1920s and '30s.* She has contributed to exhibitions at the Imperial War Museum on wartime fashions, Utility clothing, and on the Home Front, and she regularly gives talks and lectures on these and related topics. Other books by Carol Harris include *Women at War—the Home Front* (Sutton 2001), and *Women at War—in Uniform* (Sutton 2002).

INDEX